Why Are You Really Here?

Written by Nelson Brown
Illustrated by Kusum Kapat

Why Are You Really Here?
© Copyright 2025
Nelson Brown, Illustrated by Kusum Kapat Wide Woke Creations publication

All rights reserved. No part of this publication may be reproduced, distributed or transmitted in any form or by any means, including photocopying, recording, or other electronic or mechanical methods, without the prior written permission of the publisher, except in the case of brief quotations embodied in critical reviews and certain other noncommercial uses permitted by copyright law.
Although the author and publisher have made every effort to ensure that the information in this book was correct at press time, the author and publisher do not assume and hereby disclaim any liability to any party for any loss, damage, or disruption caused by errors or omissions, whether such errors or omissions result from negligence, accident, or any other cause.
Adherence to all applicable laws and regulations, including international, federal, state and local governing professional licensing, business practices, advertising, and all other aspects of doing business in the US, Canada or any other jurisdiction is the sole responsibility of the reader and consumer.
Neither the author nor the publisher assumes any responsibility or liability whatsoever on behalf of the consumer or reader of this material. Any perceived slight of any individual or organization is purely unintentional.
The resources in this book are provided for informational purposes only and should not be used to replace the specialized training and professional judgment of a health care or mental health care professional.
Neither the author nor the publisher can be held responsible for the use of the information provided within this book. Please always consult a trained professional before making any decision regarding treatment of yourself or others.

ISBN: 979-8-89109-289-1- paperback
 ISBN: 979-8-89109-290-7- ebook
ISBN: 979-8-89109-291-4- hardcover

For bulk copies of the book, or speaking engagements, please contact Wide Woke Creations at creationsbynelson@gmail.com

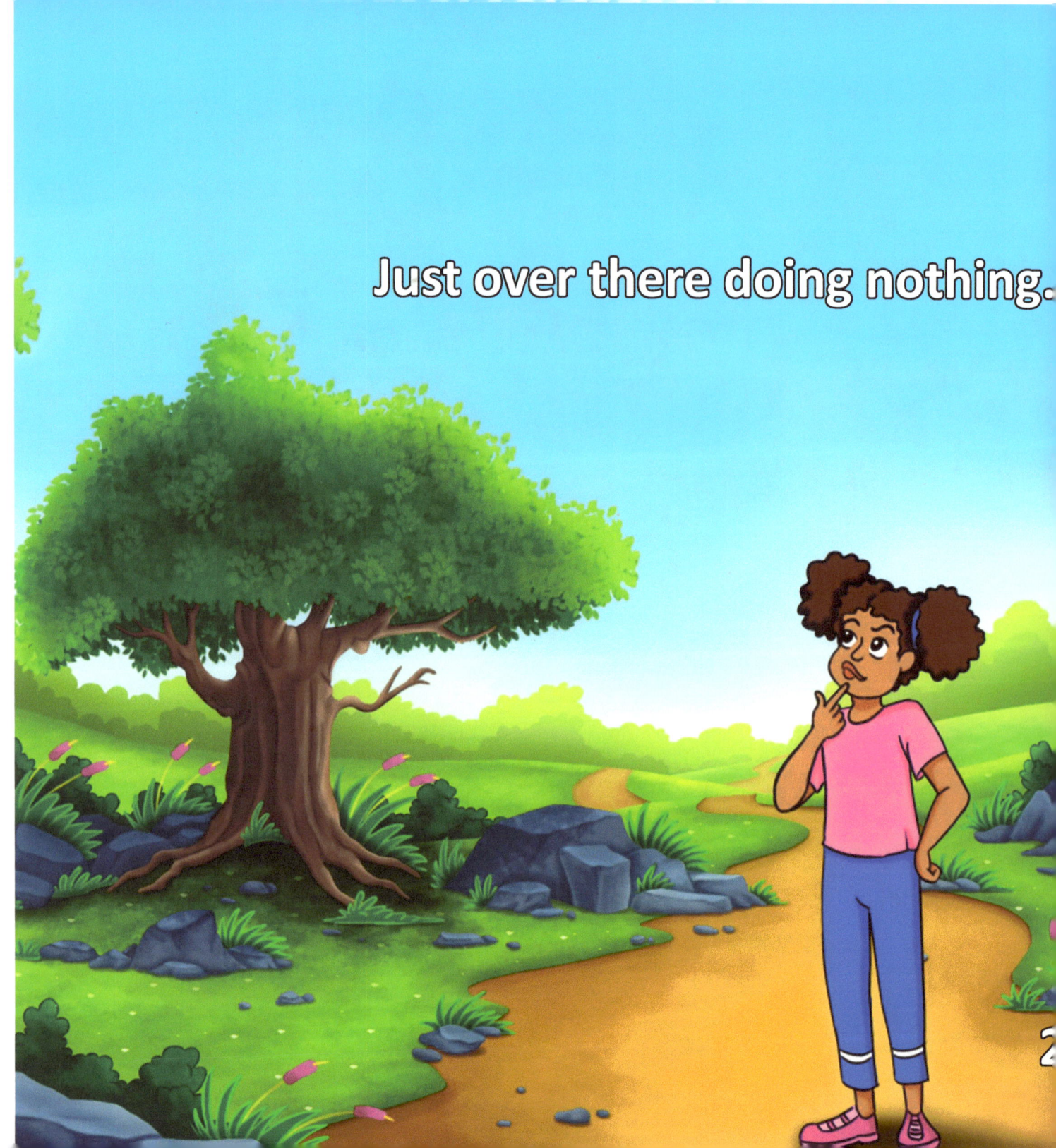

All day and night you're just standing there.

Just then, a strong wind blew in and scared the little girl.

Hello little girl! I heard everything you said. Now, you can hear me too.

Oh my! This tree is talking to me!

Yes, I am. You were wondering about my worth because you believe I just sit here every day doing nothing.

I'm sorry. I didn't mean to make you feel bad, but it seems like you do nothing at all.

It's okay. Many people think that. Do you mind if I show you what I really do every day?

Okay! I'll just have a seat here on this rock and listen.

"Purpose" is an understanding of why something or someone exists or is alive.

Oh! So, it is the reason why we are here.

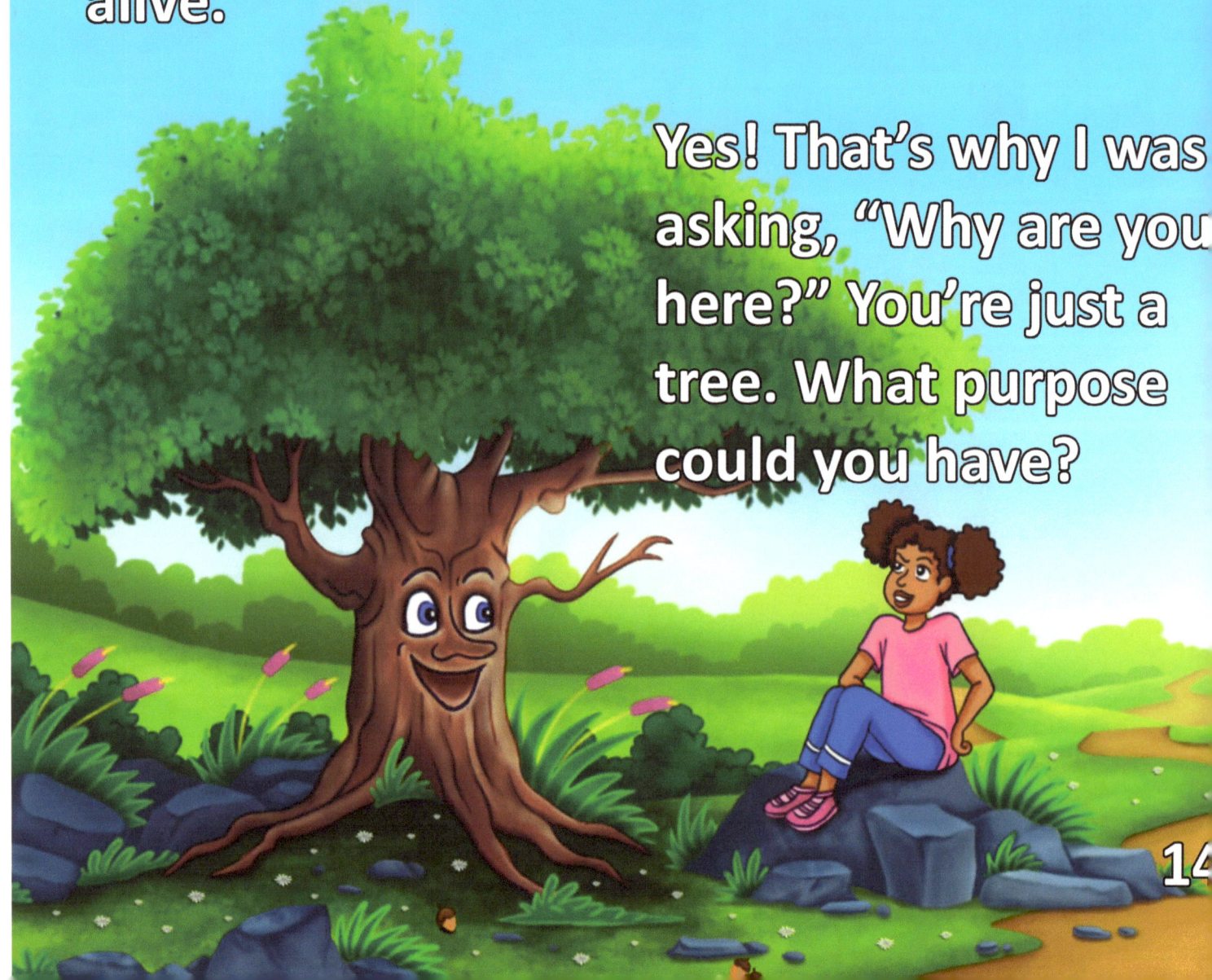

The real question you should ask yourself is, "What purpose do you have?"

Me? I'm just a little girl. I don't have a purpose yet.

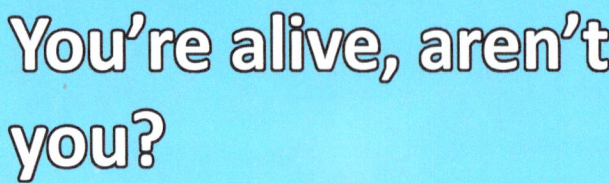

You're alive, aren't you?

Yes but, I'm so young and small. What could I possibly do at this age?

Your purpose has nothing to do with your age, size, or anything else. It is about you being your best where you are, and with who you are.

I'm not sure I understand.

To help you understand, let me first tell you about my purpose.

Thank you! That's what I wanted to know anyway!

See those ants? They depend on me for food from my leaves and fruit. It feeds their families.

Okay.

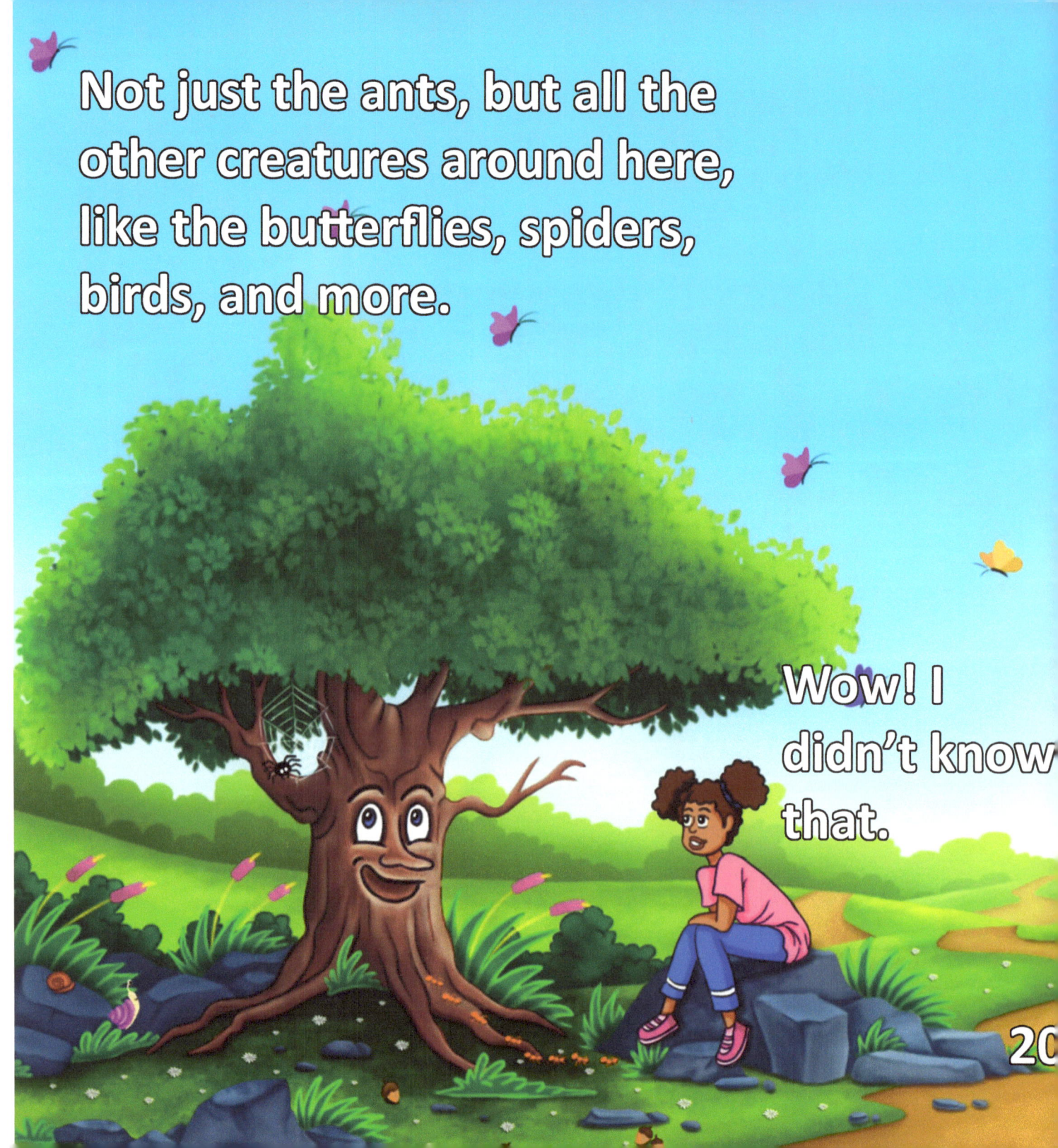

Bees and some birds build their nests in me to raise their families as well. They need a home.

You really do more than I ever imagined.

Exactly! And when you see someone in need, what do you do?

Sometimes I want to help them, but then I get scared and don't do anything.

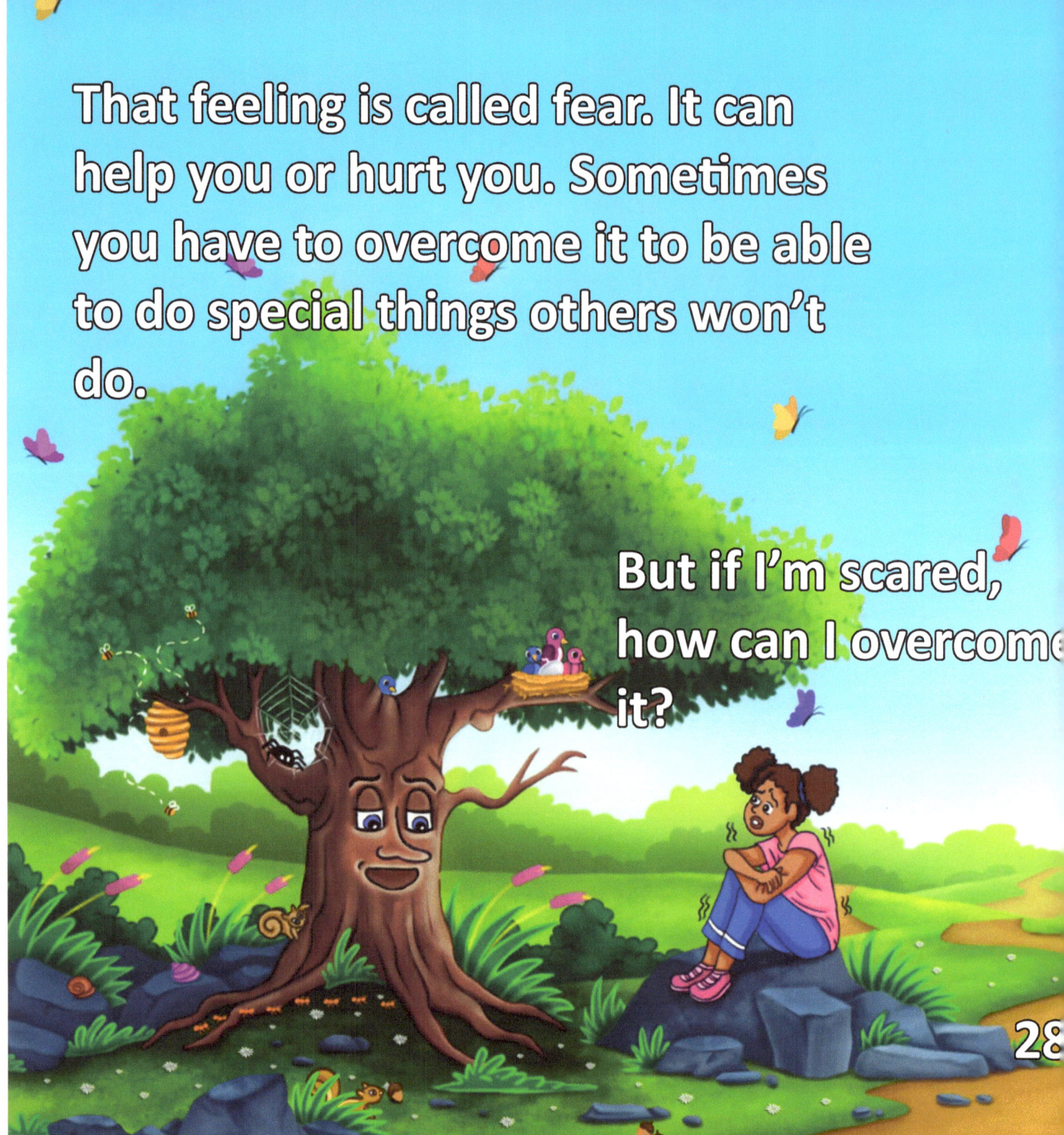

That feeling is called fear. It can help you or hurt you. Sometimes you have to overcome it to be able to do special things others won't do.

But if I'm scared, how can I overcome it?

What I can share with you is, sometimes you need to believe in something more than you fear it.

What if I don't have anything to believe in? Then what?

That is the place where you can become stuck and not do anything.

Well, if nothing happens, I won't have anything to be afraid of.

Something like that. It's not that no one wins. It more like, no one loves.

No one loves? Now, I'm more confused!

You see, purpose is doing what you love. When we live with purpose, we are showing love. Love for ourselves and love for others. When we don't, no one gets that love.

So, purpose and love go together! I get it!

Yes, they do! I do what I do wherever I am. It's my way of showing love. Love is what we do.

Showing love for myself and others gives me purpose. And I do that by what I do for myself and others.

Being helpful is a great start! As you listen more to your heart, it will show more to you as you get older.

And the more I learn, the more I can live with purpose.

And the more you live with purpose, the more you love.

And the more I love, the happier I will be, and the happier those around me will be.

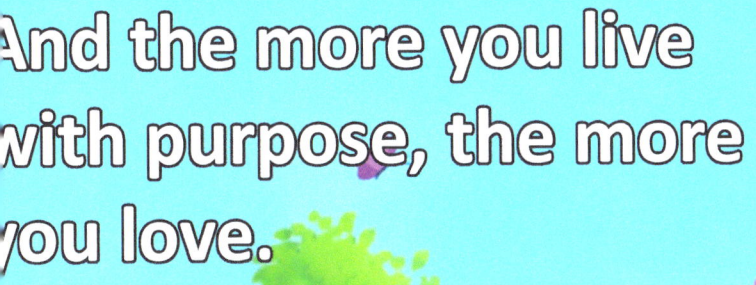

www.ingramcontent.com/pod-product-compliance
Lightning Source LLC
Chambersburg PA
CBHW041414010526
44107CB00016B/1161